CW01151589

Original title:
Snowdrift

Copyright © 2024 Swan Charm
All rights reserved.

Author: Mirell Mesipuu
ISBN HARDBACK: 978-9916-79-981-9
ISBN PAPERBACK: 978-9916-79-982-6
ISBN EBOOK: 978-9916-79-983-3

Solitude in a White Canvas

In the stillness, silence grows,
The white expanse, where no one goes.
Footsteps echo, soft and slow,
A secret realm, where dreams can flow.

Painted whispers on the frost,
A quiet peace, yet feeling lost.
Here, the heart can breathe and sigh,
In solitude, beneath the sky.

Muffled Steps on Crystal Paths

Through the glimmer, shadows glide,
Muffled steps, with nowhere to hide.
The world transformed, a sparkling sheet,
Where every move is bittersweet.

In the shimmer, secrets curl,
A dance with whispers, a silent whirl.
Every breath a crystal sound,
In this dream, where peace is found.

The Lullaby of Frozen Air

Whispers soft, in frosty breath,
A lullaby to the stillness of death.
Each note a shimmer, pure and bright,
In the embrace of the silent night.

Beneath the stars, the world turns slow,
Cradled in the winter's glow.
The air alive with dreams untold,
In the balmy chill, hearts unfold.

Veils of White in the Moonlight

The moon drapes white, a gentle sigh,
Veils of snow drift softly by.
In the hush, the world seems bare,
Wrapped in silence, lost in prayer.

Each flake a story, a fleeting glance,
A chance to dream, a wistful dance.
Under this shroud, the night aglow,
In the veils of white, we let go.

The Lullaby of Ice

Whispers drift on frozen air,
Crystals dance without a care.
Moonlight glistens, soft and pale,
Winter's song—a gentle veil.

Snowflakes tumble, swirl with grace,
Silent magic fills the space.
Nature's hush, a quiet night,
Wrapped in dreams, all feels just right.

Stars twinkle in the frosty skies,
While time slips by, the world sighs.
Sleepy shadows glide and play,
In a tranquil, icy ballet.

Echoes on a Blanket

Underneath a quilt of white,
Footsteps leave a soft, clear sight.
Whispers travel through the air,
Nature's voice, a breath of care.

Frosty whispers greet the dawn,
While the silent earth moves on.
Echoes ripple through the trees,
Carried gently by the breeze.

Every sound, a story spun,
In the glow of the rising sun.
Moments cherished, hearts entwined,
Memories woven, peace defined.

Nature's Quiet Canvas

A canvas stretched in purest white,
Brush of winter, soft and light.
Silent strokes of icy blue,
Nature's art, forever new.

Trees adorned with crystal lace,
Time stands still in this embrace.
Serenity in every glance,
Through the stillness, dreams enhance.

In this quiet, hearts can hear,
The gentle whispers drawing near.
A masterpiece that calls our eyes,
In nature's breath, a sweet surprise.

Serene Frostbound

In a land where silence reigns,
Frosty breath on window panes.
Stars above in velvet night,
Wrapped in love, the world feels right.

Through the trees, a soft wind calls,
Nature's hush, as twilight falls.
Every crystal, every light,
Fills the heart with pure delight.

Snowflakes glisten, dreams take flight,
Whispers linger, soft and slight.
In the stillness, we find peace,
Moments cherished, time's release.

Quiet Corners of a Frozen Realm

In the stillness, shadows glide,
Snowflakes dance, soft and wide.
Ancient trees stand tall and grand,
Cloaked in white, they keep the land.

Whispers echo through the night,
Moonlit paths, a silver light.
Hidden secrets stored in frost,
In this silence, nothing's lost.

A breath of winter, crisp and clear,
Lonely whispers, drawing near.
Each corner holds a tale untold,
In frozen dreams, the heart takes hold.

The gentle hush, the world's embrace,
Nature's magic in this space.
Quiet corners, peace does steal,
In frozen realms, our hearts can heal.

Glistening Whispers of Chill

Glistening whispers, the cold arrives,
With every breath, the stillness thrives.
Icicles hang like crystal tears,
Reflecting light through silent years.

Beneath the snow, the earth does sigh,
Nature's dreams beneath the sky.
Branches heavy, bending low,
With pristine coats of frosty glow.

In every flake, a story spun,
Fleeting moments, one by one.
The chill wraps round, a tender fold,
In every whisper, warmth retold.

A gentle breath, the quiet sway,
Of winter's heart at end of day.
Glistening whispers, soft and light,
Embrace the magic of the night.

Fragments of Winter's Breath

Fragments of breath in the icy air,
Each one lingers, light as prayer.
Embers of warmth in a chilly space,
Caught in the frost, a wild chase.

Furry creatures scurry and dance,
In winter's grip, they take their chance.
Under the stars, their secrets hide,
In a world that feels vast and wide.

Shadows stretch as twilight falls,
Whispers echo through the halls.
In the stillness, time stands still,
Each fragment holds a magic thrill.

The glow of fire, a beacon bright,
In the midst of the coldest night.
Fragments of joy in the frozen breath,
Life's warmth defying winter's death.

The Artistry of Ice and Air

The artistry of ice and air,
Forms the beauty that we share.
Frozen rivers, lace-like streams,
Nature's canvas, shaped by dreams.

With every glisten, stories flow,
Carved by winters, soft and slow.
A tapestry of frosty hue,
Reflects the world in colors new.

Shapes that shimmer, twist, and bend,
In this realm, shall dreams transcend.
A fleeting moment caught in time,
The essence of a winter rhyme.

As cold winds weave through trees at night,
The artistry comes to pure light.
In every breath, the chill does dance,
A fleeting, beautiful expanse.

The Call of the Cold

Whispers in the icy air,
Calling all to come and share.
Nature dons her frosty crown,
As the winter sun goes down.

Chill winds dance through barren trees,
Frosty kisses on the breeze.
Footsteps crunch on sparkling snow,
In the twilight's gentle glow.

Fires crackle, warmth inside,
While the stars begin to glide.
Wrapped in layers, hearts are bold,
Listening to the call of cold.

Enchanted Winterland

Glistening fields, a snowy sheet,
Dreams are woven at our feet.
Every flake a story told,
In this world of purest gold.

Laughter echoes, children play,
In this bright, enchanted sway.
Snowmen stand with button eyes,
Underneath the wintry skies.

Whirls of white, a mystic dance,
In this land, we find romance.
Nature's art, a scene so grand,
Welcome to this winterland.

Boughs Burdened with White

Branches droop with heavy grace,
A silent, gleaming, white embrace.
Boughs burdened, caught in time,
Nature sings, a soothing rhyme.

Softly falls the quiet snow,
Blankets all, a gentle glow.
Crisp and fresh, the air so bright,
Drapes the world in purest white.

Amidst the peace, the stillness grows,
As the evening twilight shows.
Underneath the moonlit sight,
Boughs burdened with the night.

Tranquil Winter's Breath

In the hush of snow's embrace,
Winter breathes with gentle grace.
Nature whispers, soft and clear,
In this time, the world draws near.

Silhouettes of trees stand still,
Chilled by winter's quiet thrill.
Stars above begin to gleam,
Woven in a frosty dream.

In this realm of white and gray,
Time slows down, it gently sways.
With each breath, we feel the bliss,
Of winter's tranquil, quiet kiss.

Gentle Impressions of Ice

Crystal blankets shimmer bright,
Covering the world in white.
Whispers dance upon the breeze,
Nature holds her breath with ease.

Fingers trace on frozen lakes,
Echoes of the warmth it takes.
A tender touch of winter's hand,
Marks a beauty, crisp and grand.

Glimmers catch the soft sunlight,
Casting shadows, pure and light.
Each shard sparkles, a brief glow,
Moments captured in the snow.

Silent woods, a world composed,
Among the trees, life is enclosed.
Footprints tell of journeys made,
In winter's grip, none can evade.

Chill of air, a lullaby,
As twilight's colors start to fly.
Holding close this fleeting time,
In gentle ice, a winter rhyme.

The Lattice of Winter

Snowflakes weave a frosty lace,
Adorning trees with quiet grace.
Branches bow, a heavy load,
Nature's web along the road.

Each strand glistens, pure and clear,
A tapestry that draws us near.
In the hush of coldest nights,
Stars appear like distant lights.

Wind sings softly through the boughs,
Every moment humbly vows.
To capture peace in every breath,
In the chill, we find new depth.

Moonlight bathes the world in dreams,
Softly glows, and gently gleams.
In this lattice, hearts will meet,
Finding warmth in winter's sheet.

Echoes of the past arise,
As time slips quickly past our eyes.
In this quiet, life's embrace,
We find solace in the space.

Whispers of Winter's Veil

Winter wraps the world in white,
Softly cloaked in quiet light.
Each flake falls like a gentle sigh,
Painting dreams as time drifts by.

Frosted breath upon the air,
Silent moments, rich and rare.
In the stillness, hearts align,
As whispers weave through space and time.

Bare branches reach for skies so grey,
Hoping for a sunny day.
Yet in this chill, we find our song,
In winter's hold, we still belong.

Laughter echoes through the snow,
In every flurry, joys will grow.
Children play in blissful cheer,
As the season wraps us near.

Twinkling lights in windows bright,
Bring warmth and hope to winter's night.
In every shadow, a promise waits,
Of spring's embrace, as winter hesitates.

A Blanket of Solitude

In the stillness of the night,
a whisper rides the breeze,
soft shadows wrap me tight,
   a blanket of memories.

Moonlight dances on the ground,
a silver thread of dreams,
the world outside is drowned,
in silence, so it seems.

Stars above begin to glow,
a celestial embrace,
in solitude, I flow,
finding my sacred space.

Each heartbeat is a song,
a melody of peace,
where I can feel I belong,
as worries fade and cease.

In this quiet, I am free,
untouched by the day's strife,
a moment just for me,
a dance of calm in life.

The Silent Tapestry

Woven threads of time abound,
a tapestry of grace,
in every stitch, a sound,
a quiet, warm embrace.

Colors blend in every hue,
a story, softly told,
of dreams and hopes that grew,
in patterns rich and bold.

The whispers of the loom,
a gentle, rhythmic flow,
in shadows, light finds room,
where memories can grow.

Each fiber holds a tale,
a journey shared in peace,
a harmony that prevails,
a tapestry's release.

In silence, I can glean,
the beauty of this art,
a woven, sacred scene,
an echo of the heart.

Shimmering Frostbind

Morning breaks with frost's embrace,
a shimmering delight,
crystals form a delicate trace,
as day dissolves the night.

Each blade of grass aglow,
a sparkling veil of white,
a world transformed below,
a wondrous, glistening sight.

The air is crisp and clear,
a breath of winter's charm,
with every step, I hear,
a song, serene and calm.

Nature's canvas, pure and bright,
a fleeting, icy bond,
where shadows dance in light,
a shimmering response.

In this space, my heart untwines,
a beauty pure and blind,
in winter's soft confines,
my spirit, gently shined.

Frosted Secrets

Beneath the frost, dark secrets lie,
a world draped in disguise,
where hidden truths softly sigh,
ya symphony of lies.

Each flake that falls, a story told,
a whisper in the chill,
of tales that time cannot withhold,
a lingering thrill.

The trees stand tall, with branches bare,
a watchful, ancient gaze,
they guard what few would dare,
the echoes of past days.

In silence, secrets intertwine,
a dance beneath the sky,
with every breath, I feel the line,
where dreams and shadows lie.

Cloaked in frost, my heart takes flight,
a journey deep and wide,
in the stillness of the night,
in frost, my truths reside.

A World Wrapped in Quietude

The soft murmur of dawn breaks,
A gentle hush cloaks the trees,
Whispers float on the cool breeze,
Nature's sigh, a sweet embrace.

The daffodils bow in grace,
Bathed in dew, a sparkling sheen,
Clouds drift lazily, serene,
Painting skies in a tender space.

Footsteps lost in tender trails,
Birdsongs dance through the quiet,
Every heartbeat feels the might,
As peace envelops like soft veils.

A brook babbles softly nearby,
Crisp leaves crackle underfoot,
Moments linger, deeply rooted,
In stillness where dreams can fly.

Here time pauses, slows its pace,
In this world, life's worries fade,
A refuge within the glade,
Wrapped in quiet's warm embrace.

Hushed Secrets in White Silence

Blankets of snow gently fall,
Whispers cover the sleeping ground,
In this stillness, secrets abound,
Silent stories waiting to call.

Moonlight glistens on the drifts,
Stars shimmer in frosty skies,
In the night, the magic lies,
Touched by winter's softest gifts.

Branches wear a crystal crown,
Ice crystals glimmer in the glow,
The world slows, drifting in slow,
Nature's peace, her softest gown.

Details hidden, softly blurred,
Each step crunches with secrets told,
In this realm of white and gold,
A sanctuary, quietly stirred.

Here, silence holds the heart close,
Breath made visible in the air,
In winter's own, a rich affair,
Hushed in beauty, we can chose.

Echoes in the Winter Air

Frosty whispers kiss the trees,
Chill hangs heavy in the glow,
The world adorned in whites and browns,
Echoes dance where few can see.

Voices carried on the wind,
Stories shared beneath the moon,
In the night, a gentle tune,
Fleeting thoughts we've yet to send.

Footprints mark the path we've tread,
Each one tells a tale in snow,
Silent witnesses, they know,
The dreams and wishes left unsaid.

In every breath, a cloud appears,
The cold cradles our every sigh,
Hearts warm despite the frosty cry,
In winter's chill, we shed our fears.

Eager dawn breaks through the haze,
With soft sunlight, shadows play,
But echoes of the night will stay,
In memories, wrapped in frost's embrace.

The Journey of Wandering Frost

Each night, the frost creeps in slow,
Drawing lines on window panes,
Her delicate dance, no refrains,
In silence, the world's new glow.

With sunrise, she bids goodbye,
Leaving whispers on the grass,
A fleeting touch, as hours pass,
A soft farewell, a lingering sigh.

She wisps through forests, wild and free,
Embracing every branch and stone,
In her path, silver gems are sown,
Nature's art for all to see.

Through valleys deep and mountains high,
Frost travels far, both near and wide,
In each crevice, secrets reside,
A transient beauty that won't die.

So let the chill wrap round your heart,
For in her touch, there's magic found,
A gentle peace, a soothing sound,
The journey of frost, an artful part.

Dances of Chill Under a Soft Moon

Beneath the gleam of silver night,
The whispers of the frost take flight.
In gentle flurries, shadows glide,
While secrets of the dark reside.

Snowflakes twirl in frigid air,
As dreams entwine the silent square.
The earth wears white as softest lace,
Each breath a dance, a fleeting grace.

Moonlight pools on icy streams,
Where echoes linger in soft dreams.
The world holds still, a breath held tight,
In the stillness, hearts alight.

Branches bow with burdens rare,
Nature's canvas, pure and fair.
Footprints left in softest snow,
Tell stories only night does know.

With every step, the chill ignites,
A symphony in winter's sights.
Together lost in soft moon's glow,
We dance along, the night our show.

The Breath of a Glacial Heart

In frozen realms where silence reigns,
The heart of ice beats, unrestrained.
Each sigh a gust from ages past,
A rhythm strong, forever cast.

Mountains loom with regal grace,
Their majesty, a cold embrace.
Where streams are born from ancient tears,
They carry tales of countless years.

With every pulse, the world does freeze,
And time itself bows to the breeze.
Whispers travel through the cold,
In glacial paths, our stories told.

The light refracts in prisms grand,
As nature weaves her gentle hand.
Each sparkle sings, a frozen sigh,
Underneath the endless sky.

Beneath the weight of winter's song,
The earth endures, steadfast and strong.
In the breath of cold, we find our way,
In frozen hearts, we long to stay.

In the Embrace of Winter's Quiet

When twilight falls, the world grows still,
Each flake descends with dreamy will.
Underneath the starry sweep,
The earth sighs low, a gentle sleep.

Pine trees stand in solemn rows,
Their branches dressed in frozen bows.
The silence hums a soothing tune,
In winter's hold, beneath the moon.

A blanket white, so deep and soft,
Hides secrets of the world aloft.
The air is crisp, the night is clear,
In every breath, the frost draws near.

Softly now, the shadows creep,
As nature whispers, dreams to keep.
In every corner, stillness grows,
A tranquil grace that nature shows.

From icy ponds to valleys wide,
In winter's heart, our hopes reside.
Together wrapped in tender night,
In winter's glow, we find delight.

The Serene Chill of a Frozen Dream

In the stillness of night,
Stars twinkle like frost,
Dreams whisper soft secrets,
In shadows, they are lost.

Beneath a blanket of white,
Silent echoes reside,
Time drifts slowly away,
In the chill, we confide.

Figures dance in the mist,
Frozen laughter in air,
A world wrapped in crystal,
Delightfully rare.

Night's embrace cradles all,
With a sigh, we relent,
A frozen dream unfolds,
Past the moments we spent.

Here in this quiet space,
We find peace in the cold,
Wrapped in a gentle shroud,
A warmth yet to be told.

Cold Journeys to Forgotten Places

Tracks lead to the unknown,
Snowflakes fall like tears,
Footsteps in the silence,
Through the weight of the years.

Whispers of those once here,
Echo in the pale night,
Each breath is felt anew,
In the fading twilight.

Ghosts of memories roam,
In the crisp, biting air,
Shadows of who we were,
Paint stories everywhere.

Each journey bears a truth,
In the frost, we are found,
A connection to the past,
In the silence profound.

Through the trails of winter,
We carry our own fight,
Finding warmth in this cold,
As we step into light.

Beneath the Surface

Layers of ice conceal,
The stories of the deep,
Silently they dream on,
Where secrets dare to keep.

Ripples break the stillness,
A touch of life appears,
What lies beneath the frost,
Holds both joy and fears.

In the dark, shadows linger,
Silent songs ebb and flow,
A world that breathes beneath,
Where few will ever go.

The surface hides the truth,
Yet charms us with its grace,
A mystery unfolding,
In this frozen place.

Above, the sky whispers,
While beneath, silence stirs,
Connecting paths of life,
In the cold, we confer.

Whispers Linger

In the garden of frost,
Whispers carry on air,
Each breath a gentle sigh,
Each moment laid bare.

Echoes of laughter drift,
Through the chill of the night,
A chorus of memories,
In the silver moonlight.

The branches sway softly,
Cradled by the cold breeze,
Every rustle a secret,
Carried through barren trees.

Whispers linger softly,
In the heart of the freeze,
A song of longing calls,
Beneath the darkened leaves.

Held tight in the silence,
Promises float like dreams,
In the quiet, we find,
The warmth of our themes.

Windswept Silence of the Tempest

Winds howl through the night,
A tempest sings its song,
Nature's fierce embrace grips,
Where shadows roam along.

Clouds gather like whispers,
In a brewing dismay,
The air is thick with tension,
As night turns into day.

Beneath the raging skies,
Silence echoes so loud,
A heartbeat in the storm,
Lost within the crowd.

Each gust carries meaning,
In a dance of despair,
Yet through chaos, we see,
A beauty lurking there.

When the storm finally calms,
And the raging winds cease,
We find strength in the silence,
And in that, we find peace.

Solitary Frosted Dreams

Amidst the silent whispering night,
Frosty breath clings to shadows tight.
A world adorned in white and gleam,
Hopes drift softly like a dream.

Barren trees in slumber steep,
Crystals glow where secrets keep.
Each breath a fleeting glimpse of peace,
In solitude, the troubles cease.

Underneath the starlit dome,
Nature finds a quiet home.
Frozen thoughts drift on the air,
Solitude, a gentle care.

The moonlight paints the earth in grace,
Each step taken, a slow embrace.
Whispers echo, soft and clear,
In frosted dreams, I hold you near.

Shadows Beneath the Glacial Sky

Beneath a pale and frozen gaze,
Shadows dance in winter's haze.
Silent figures move with care,
Ghostly forms illuminate the air.

Icicles hang, a silver thread,
Casting dreams of warmth ahead.
The cold wraps tight, yet hearts ignite,
In whispered tales of winter's night.

Stars twinkle through the icy mist,
Each one holds a secret kissed.
Frosted paths lead to the unknown,
In shadows where the wild hearts roam.

Through the night, a soft refrain,
Melodies of whispered pain.
Yet hope rises, soft and shy,
In the shadows beneath the sky.

Shimmering Threads of Winter's Weave

Threads of silver, soft and light,
Weave a tapestry of night.
Each glimmer holds a story told,
In winter's grasp, our dreams unfold.

Winds whisper secrets, ancient, clear,
Frosty tendrils draw us near.
Nature's art, a quiet song,
In sparkling threads, we all belong.

A delicate dance in the moon's embrace,
Seasons blend in a timeless space.
With every stitch, the stillness grows,
A shimmered world we all compose.

Fingers trace the woven lace,
In the cold, we find our place.
Together, we weave through night's fair veil,
In shimmering grace, we shall prevail.

The Canvas of a Frozen Heart

In winter's clutch, emotions freeze,
A canvas stretched by chilling breeze.
Colors muted, shades of blue,
In frost, the heart finds something new.

Life's brush strokes are soft yet bold,
In frozen silence, stories unfold.
Each heartbeat paints with gentle care,
An artful dance in the bitter air.

Frigid dreams on a canvas bright,
Brush of love, warmth ignites.
In each layer, memories lie,
A painted truth beneath the sky.

Though winter comes with icy breath,
In frosted art, we conquer death.
The frozen heart beats strong and clear,
In every stroke, we persevere.

Chilled Silence

In the depths of winter night,
The world rests without a sound.
Snowflakes fall, a gentle flight,
In soft blankets, peace is found.

Moonlight shines on frosty ground,
Whispers of the cold air breathe.
Nature sleeps, a still surround,
As time weaves its quiet weave.

Footsteps crunch on glistening snow,
Echoes dance through frozen trees.
In shadows, secrets start to grow,
As heartbeats sync with winter's freeze.

Stars above in velvet spread,
Twinkle down like dreams untold.
As silence wraps like a soft thread,
The night enfolds both calm and bold.

Beneath the blanket, warmth abides,
A hearth that glows, a fire's embrace.
In chilled silence, love resides,
Together in this sacred space.

The Dance of Flakes

Twisting, turning through the air,
Snowflakes waltz, a soft ballet.
Spirits lift without a care,
In their hush, they leap and sway.

Each one unique, a crafted grace,
Delicate in their frosted flight.
Frosted lace in winter's embrace,
As day drifts softly into night.

Whirling dreams in icy streams,
A dance that time cannot confine.
Below the moon, like whispered themes,
They spiral down, a spark divine.

Children laugh, their faces bright,
As flakes alight on coats and hair.
Every twirl a pure delight,
In snowy realms beyond compare.

The ground adorned with nature's art,
A canvas blank transformed anew.
In this ballet, joy takes part,
As winter paints a world in blue.

Frozen Whispers

In the stillness of the frost,
Nature whispers soft and low.
With every breath, a tale is tossed,
Of winter's touch, a timeless flow.

Branches bare, a silver lace,
Crystals shimmer, light ensnares.
In their grip, the moon's embrace,
A symphony of quiet prayers.

Hushed winds drift like lover's sighs,
Through the pines and oaks they weave.
In the dark, where secrets lie,
Frozen whispers shall never leave.

Echoes speak in chilling tones,
Life pauses, wrapped in cold's grace.
Among the trees, the night moans,
In frozen bliss, we find our place.

Winter's breath, a soft caress,
In stillness, magic finds its home.
In frozen whispers, hearts confess,
No longer are we bound to roam.

Crystal Coverlet

A blanket spread of glistening white,
Cocooned in beauty, the earth reclines.
Underneath, the world sleeps tight,
In dreams spun from the cold confines.

Sparkling gems on every bough,
Nature wears her finest dress.
In winter's arms, we take a vow,
To cherish this pure happiness.

Footprints trace a tale of joy,
As laughter pierces through the chill.
With every leap, like a child's toy,
We revel in the magic still.

Frost-kissed air and glowing light,
A crystal coverlet shines bright.
In whispers, shadows dance in flight,
As starlit dreams embrace the night.

In the hush of falling stars,
We hold together, hearts entwined.
With every breath, our spirits spar,
Underneath this cover we find.

A World Paused in Chill

The trees are silent, dressed in white,
A blanket of frost, a shimmering sight.
Footsteps hush upon the ground,
In this calm, peace is found.

Breath hangs like clouds in the air,
Each moment still, a frozen stare.
Time seems to pause, to hold on tight,
In the heart of this winter night.

The stars twinkle in the sky,
As soft winds whisper a lullaby.
Nature sleeps, draped in dreams,
Under soft moonlight beams.

Windows glow with a warm embrace,
Filled with laughter and grace.
Outside, the world is dressed in chill,
Inside, hearts dance and thrill.

Beneath the ice, life awakes,
In silence, the world gently shakes.
Awaiting spring's softest touch,
A world paused in chill, it means so much.

Frosty Reflections

Ripples dance on the frozen lake,
Mirrors of dreams, softly awake.
Trees stretch tall, with branches bare,
In the stillness, secrets flare.

Crystal droplets hang like gems,
Nature's art, the frosty hems.
Every shadow holds a tale,
As winds weave through the icy veil.

Footprints lead where hearts can roam,
In this chill, we find our home.
Glistening paths pull us near,
In frosty reflections, all is clear.

The air tastes sharp, a sweet embrace,
Each breath a plume, time's gentle pace.
Finding joy in the frozen scene,
Life's beauty wrapped in silver sheen.

With every breath, we reminisce,
Moments captured, the winter's kiss.
As day fades into night's gentle hold,
Frosty reflections, memories bold.

The Stillness Within

Amidst the frost, the world seems still,
A quiet calm that time can't kill.
The flurry fades to silent grace,
In this moment, we find our place.

Soft whispers of falling snow,
Encircle hearts, like rivers slow.
Each flake unique, a story spun,
In the stillness, life's begun.

Breath mingles with the crisp, clear air,
A gentle reminder that we care.
Moments freeze, yet feelings flow,
In this silence, we come to know.

Beneath the frost, a heartbeat lies,
Waiting for warmth to rise.
The stillness within calls out to us,
Embracing winter, in quiet trust.

As stars twinkle in the night,
The world bathed soft in silver light.
The stillness within, a cherished gift,
In winter's embrace, our spirits lift.

Lattice of Ice

Intricate webs of glistening frost,
Nature's beauty, never lost.
Each crystal a fragment of the sun,
In the lattice, all is one.

Branches lace against the sky,
Echoes of winter whispered by.
Shapes are formed, both sharp and kind,
In the lattice, we seek to find.

Reflections dance on surfaces clear,
Silent joy, without fear.
Gentle patterns, harmonious flow,
In this lattice, time moves slow.

Each moment captured, a fleeting glance,
In frozen silence, we take a chance.
Winter weaves a tale so bright,
In the lattice of ice, pure delight.

Embrace the chill, let wonder in,
Under the frost, life will begin.
The lattice holds a world anew,
In every crystal, dreams come true.

Through the Frosty Veil

A silver mist hangs low,
The trees adorned in white,
Footprints soft in snow,
A world draped in twilight.

Branches bend and sway,
Whispers of the breeze,
In the heart of day,
Nature's gentle freeze.

Silent hues unfold,
In the crisp of air,
Tales of winter told,
Every breath a prayer.

The stars begin to blink,
As the night draws near,
In the frost we think,
Of dreams without fear.

Underneath the moon,
Our hearts beat in time,
With a soft, sweet tune,
Winter's quiet rhyme.

A Whisper of Ice

A gentle caress,
On the frozen ground,
Soft whispers confess,
The stillness around.

Frosted windows gleam,
In the pale moonlight,
Each breath a soft dream,
Captured in the night.

Shadows dance and play,
Under silver skies,
Lost in shades of gray,
Where the quiet lies.

The world holds its breath,
In this chilled embrace,
Nature pauses death,
To find its own grace.

Hear the silence call,
In the icy glow,
Winter's gentle thrall,
As the cold winds blow.

Secrets of the Winter Night

Underneath the stars,
In the velvet sky,
Winter's frozen bars,
Hold the whispers high.

Crystals in the air,
Glisten like the dreams,
Veils of frosted care,
Shine with silver gleams.

Every breath a cloud,
Mingling with the dark,
Silent, solemn crowd,
Where the shadows spark.

Hushed beneath the weight,
Of the night so deep,
Time will softly wait,
In its tranquil sweep.

Secrets left untold,
In the chilly breeze,
Winter's gentle hold,
Brings us to our knees.

Lull in the Blizzard

The winds howl their song,
Through the whirling snow,
In this dance we long,
For the warmth to grow.

Blankets, fresh and white,
Covering the earth,
In the soft moonlight,
We find winter's hearth.

Quiet fills the air,
As the storm recedes,
With a gentle care,
It sows winter's seeds.

Each flake tells a tale,
Of the skies above,
In this frosty veil,
Nature's gift of love.

Cradled by the night,
With our dreams in tow,
Here we'll hold on tight,
Through the blizzard's flow.

Hidden Pathways

In shadows deep, the secrets lie,
A winding trail beneath the sky.
The trees, they bend, in whispered song,
Where few have walked, they still belong.

Footsteps soft on mossy stone,
Each twist and turn, a world unknown.
The silence holds a magic rare,
A hidden path, beyond compare.

Beneath the leaves, the pulse of earth,
Awakens echoes of rebirth.
With every step, the heart beats fast,
While time forgets, the moments last.

In twilight's glow, the path abounds,
With mysteries and whispered sounds.
The stars, they guide like ancient lore,
To places dreamed, forevermore.

So wander on, and lose your way,
In hidden realms where shadows play.
For in this maze, you may just find,
The truths that linger, unconfined.

Whispers Beneath the Surface

Ripples dance upon the stream,
Secrets flow like fleeting dreams.
In hushed tones, the waters speak,
Of buried tales, both strong and weak.

Underneath, where shadows coil,
Life awakens from its toil.
Silken threads of fate entwine,
In depths where light is hard to find.

Listen close to nature's hum,
A symphony that speaks to some.
Beneath the calm, storms often brew,
Whispers deep, that pull us through.

Each glance beneath, a world exists,
Where silence hugs, and movement twists.
The surface still, yet vibrant life,
Hides scars of love and ancient strife.

Take a breath, immerse your soul,
In watery depths, we become whole.
For with each whisper, we shall see,
The layers that define you and me.

Glacial Dreams

Upon the ice, a stillness reigns,
Where crystal shards hold nature's chains.
In pale blue light, a world seems vast,
Echoes of winter, forever cast.

Softly gliding, the frozen eyes,
Beneath the surface, beauty lies.
Yearning hearts in silence weep,
As shadows dance in slumber deep.

Frozen whispers on the breeze,
Carry tales of ancient seas.
Each jagged peak, a solemn guard,
Past mysteries where dreams are marred.

In every crevice, stories freeze,
Of wandering souls and restless seas.
Trapped in time, yet boldly gleam,
A perfect place for glacial dreams.

So wander through this frosty land,
Where ice and spirit hand in hand.
For in these chambers, cold yet bright,
Lie glacial dreams wrapped in pure light.

Resplendent in White

The world adorned in winter's veil,
A tapestry of white, so pale.
Each flake a story, soft and light,
As nature whispers, pure delight.

Mountains crowned with icy grace,
Reflections caught in winter's face.
A murmured peace, the heart's embrace,
In silence found, we find our place.

Beneath the snow, life holds its breath,
The land transformed, a dance with death.
Yet spring awaits, just out of sight,
With hope that glimmers, faint but bright.

Children laugh where hearths ignite,
Building dreams, in snow so white.
A sparkling realm where joy's reborn,
In every drift, a tale is worn.

So let us walk this path of dreams,
Where winter sings in silvery gleams.
Wrapped in warmth, though cold winds bite,
We are resplendent, pure in white.

The Crystal Archive

In the vaults of time, they gleam,
Whispers of ages, a silent dream.
Each fragment holds a secret bright,
Captured in glass, a frozen light.

Memories trapped in fragile stone,
Echoes of life, where seeds are sown.
Pages of history, soft and clear,
Each crystal tale, a voice so dear.

Guardians of moments, they quietly sigh,
Reflecting the world as days roll by.
Beneath the shimmer, shadows dance,
A mosaic of stories, a timeless trance.

Underneath the surface, secrets dwell,
In the heart of silence, they gently swell.
Infinite beauty within each shard,
In the crystal archive, forever marred.

Glimmers of wisdom reside in sight,
The past unfurls in spectral light.
With every gaze, a journey starts,
In the crystal archive, we find our hearts.

Moments of Pure White

A blanket of snow drapes the land,
Soft whispers of winter, a gentle hand.
Each flake a story, unique in flight,
Moments of pure white, a visual delight.

Silence envelops, a tranquil spell,
Footprints leading to a frozen well.
Breath forms clouds in the biting air,
Yet within this chill, the warmth we share.

Branches adorned with crystalline grace,
Nature's artistry in every place.
Time seems to pause in this sacred glow,
Moments of stillness begin to flow.

Children's laughter, a joyful sound,
As snowballs form and tumble down.
The world transformed in a gleaming sight,
In moments of pure white, hearts take flight.

As twilight falls, a silver hue,
Stars emerge in the canvas blue.
Together we gather, under moonlight,
In these moments of pure white, love shines bright.

The Shimmering Veil

Through the mist, a soft glow brews,
A veil of shimmer, a dance of hues.
Secrets cloaked in silken threads,
Entwined in whispers, where wonder treads.

Behind the curtain, dreams unfold,
Stories of heartache and tales untold.
Each shimmer holds a wish in flight,
The shimmering veil, a canvas of light.

Glistening pathways in twilight's embrace,
Illuminated trails, a magical space.
Breath of the night wraps us tight,
As shadows and sparkle weave, ignite.

In the silent moments, we find our way,
Through the shimmering veil, we'll dare to stay.
Hope flickers softly, a distant star,
Guiding our souls, no matter how far.

With every step, the veil draws near,
A promise of dreams, dispelling fear.
Together we wander, hand in hand,
Through the shimmering veil, our love will stand.

Unfurling Chill

The morning breaks with a frosty breath,
Nature awakens, in silence, it's death.
Chill in the air, a whispering breeze,
Unfurling shadows dance through the trees.

Each droplet glistens on blades of grass,
A moment of beauty, as seasons pass.
Under the twilight, frost takes its stand,
Unfurling chill, with a touch so grand.

Footprints cover the paths once known,
A trail of warmth where chill has grown.
As daylight fades, the world turns gray,
In unfurling chill, the warmth slips away.

Wisps of fog rise from valleys below,
Nature in slumber, swathed in snow.
The quiet hum of the earth's soft sigh,
In unfurling chill, the night draws nigh.

Embrace the cold, let the stillness sink,
In the heart of winter, we pause and think.
Beauty lies in the frost's gentle thrill,
In this soft season of unfurling chill.

Mirror of the Morning Sun

In the dawn's embrace, shadows fade,
A golden light begins to cascade.
Whispers of dawn greet the day,
In warmth and grace, worries drift away.

Reflections dance on still waters,
Nature's palette, as beauty proffers.
Waves of color paint the skies,
Brightened hearts and hopeful sighs.

Each ray carries dreams anew,
A canvas painted in vibrant hue.
The sun ascends, a watchful guide,
Awakening life, with arms spread wide.

Morning glories stretch and bloom,
Chasing away remnants of gloom.
In this moment, peace is spun,
Life's tapestry, a journey begun.

So linger here, let the warmth unfold,
In the mirror of dawn, stories told.
Embrace the light, let it run free,
In the mirror, we find harmony.

Crystal Threnody

In winter's hush, the crystals gleam,
Fractured whispers of a broken dream.
Each droplet weeps a tale of old,
Of love's embrace and hearts turned cold.

Ghostly echoes in the chill,
Memories dance, but time stands still.
A sorrowed song the trees lament,
In silence deep, their voices bent.

Beneath the frost, the earth sleeps tight,
Dreams untold await the light.
Yet shadows linger, hope be lost,
In crystal prisons, souls are tossed.

Nature's sigh, so soft and frail,
Paints the heart with a mournful veil.
In every shard, a tear concealed,
A bittersweet love forever healed.

Yet spring shall break this icy hold,
With golden sun and warmth untold.
Though threnodies may pierce the air,
In hope's embrace, we find repair.

The Story Beneath

Beneath the surface, whispers speak,
Unseen worlds where shadows leak.
In every stone, a tale imbued,
Of ancient hearts, of dreams pursued.

The roots entwine, a hidden thread,
In silence deep, the past is fed.
Bound by time, yet free to roam,
In the soil, we find our home.

The winds carry secrets, soft and low,
Of lives once lived, where rivers flow.
Each echo holds a memory still,
Of laughter shared, of sacred thrill.

Nature weaves a tapestry grand,
Stories etched by time's own hand.
In each leaf's flutter, a journey told,
Of fleeting moments, precious as gold.

So delve beneath, with heart open wide,
In the layers of life, let truth abide.
For within us all, stories reside,
A symphony played on fate's great tide.

Frosty Portraits

In the stillness of a winter's night,
Frosty portraits emerge in soft light.
Each crystal etched upon the glass,
A fleeting moment that cannot last.

They capture whispers of times long passed,
Memories fragile, yet held steadfast.
In every twirl, a dance of fate,
A visual echo we contemplate.

Within the chill, emotions freeze,
Nature's artistry, a silent tease.
A canvas born from chilly breath,
Each formation, a hint of death.

Yet in this beauty, life finds a way,
To sparkle and shimmer in shades of gray.
Frosty portraits reveal the heart,
In winter's grasp, we're kept apart.

Beneath the frost, the earth is alive,
Waiting for warmth, for dreams to revive.
So paint your moments, let them unfold,
In frosty portraits, life's stories told.

Frosted Elegance

Amidst the silent trees, so still,
A shimmering layer makes them thrill.
Gentle whispers through the night,
Draped in elegance, pure and white.

Softly sparkling on every ground,
A frozen beauty, profoundly bound.
Crystal diamonds catching light,
Nature's treasure, a stunning sight.

Beneath the stars, the earth's sweet grace,
Frost paints the world, a soft embrace.
Each breath a cloud in the chill air,
A canvas crafted with utmost care.

Footsteps crunch on the icy path,
Echoes of winter's soft aftermath.
In this realm where silence reigns,
Frosted elegance, beauty remains.

With every dawn, the sun will rise,
Melting kisses from winter skies.
Yet in our hearts, we hold the dream,
Of frosty nights, a silver gleam.

Nature's Frozen Poetry

In the stillness of a frozen morn,
Nature's prose is lovingly born.
Snowflakes drift on the gentle breeze,
A tapestry woven through bare trees.

Words unspoken in the winter hush,
Soft white blankets, calming the rush.
Every flake a story untold,
Each tiny crystal, a marvel of old.

The brook lies quiet, a mirrored glass,
Reflecting white skies as time does pass.
Nature whispers in this silent breath,
The poetry of life and of death.

A verse of frost on the meadow's cheek,
Quiet moments, where all seems meek.
Yet in this stillness, life holds strong,
In winter's grip, we all belong.

From dawn till dusk, the scenes will shift,
Nature's beauty, a precious gift.
In frozen silence, we find the key,
To understand life's sweet mystery.

Twilight in White

As twilight falls on a snowy eve,
A blanket whispers, soft as a weave.
Moonlight dances on frosted peaks,
In this hush, the world gently speaks.

Shadows lurk beneath the steel gray,
While stars peek through, ready to play.
The landscape glows in a tranquil light,
Wrapped in wonder, the heart takes flight.

Footprints lead to a distant dream,
In the stillness, the heart may beam.
Whispers of night wrap us in song,
Twilight in white, where we belong.

Glistening snowflakes kiss the ground,
With every heartbeat, peace is found.
In this moment, time stands still,
Embracing the joy, the winter chill.

Tomorrow brings its own new grace,
But tonight we find our sacred space.
In twilight's arms, we softly sway,
Bathed in white, we drift away.

The Frost's Tender Touch

A gentle kiss on winter's breath,
The frost bestows a touch of depth.
Nature shimmers in the quiet glow,
Wrapped in secrets only the cold can know.

Each branch adorned like a silver crown,
Soft whispers fall, the world slows down.
The grass lies still beneath its guise,
A frosty blanket hides the earth's sighs.

In morning light, a soft embrace,
Frost paints magic in every place.
A glisten in the eye of dawn,
Awakens beauty, gently drawn.

Through frosted panes, the world feels near,
Each icy breath, a moment dear.
A tender touch, a love so bold,
Winter's charm, in whispers told.

As night descends with a quiet grace,
Frost holds the magic in its embrace.
With dreams of thaw, the warmth will grow,
Yet frosted dreams will always flow.

Beneath the Layer of Frost

Beneath the layer of frost it sleeps,
Whispers of warmth in silence creeps.
Hidden dreams in the icy sheen,
Nature's calm, serene and clean.

The branches bow with weighted grace,
A frozen world, a soft embrace.
Crystal designs twinkle and shine,
Nature's art, pure and divine.

In shadows deep, the cold winds sigh,
Echoes of life where spirits lie.
The ground, a quilt of white delight,
Glistens softly in the night.

Snowflakes dance on a fleeting breath,
With each sweep, a story of death.
Yet life renews beneath this dome,
Awaiting spring to call it home.

Beneath the layer, life does await,
A promise kept, a chance, a fate.
So here we stand, in awe and trust,
Beneath the layer of frozen dust.

Secrets Hidden in the Frozen Crust

Secrets hidden in the frozen crust,
Whispers of ages, still and just.
Where shadows dance and silence reigns,
Memories linger, bound in chains.

Beneath each flake and icy veil,
Untold tales of the winter's trail.
A canvas bright with stories old,
In every shard, a world unfolds.

Beneath the frost, the earth's heartbeat,
Nature rests, embracing defeat.
Yet in that stillness, life does thrive,
In quiet corners, dreams arrive.

Hidden deep within the freeze,
Lies a magic that stirs with ease.
Each chilly gust, a gentle nudge,
To wake the warmth beneath the grudge.

Secrets waiting in the snow's embrace,
Timeless echoes, a sacred space.
In frozen crust, the hope framed right,
Awaits the dawn, and spring's first light.

A Retreat into Frigid Fantasies

A retreat into frigid fantasies,
A world wrapped in winter's remedies.
Soft whispers call from snowy lanes,
Where silence flows through frosty veins.

Dreams take flight on a swirling breeze,
Painting visions in fir and trees.
Every breath, a cloud of grace,
Each heartbeat, time's tender embrace.

Glistening fields beneath the moon,
Dance with shadows, a frosty tune.
Nature weaves through the chilly air,
Spinning tales from moments rare.

In the hush of night, splendor lies,
Beneath the stars, a spark that flies.
A retreat into worlds untold,
Where frigid fantasies unfold.

The winter's breath, a soft caress,
Carries dreams with a gentle press.
In this realm of crystal light,
Magic blossoms, pure and bright.

The Tapestry of the Winter's End

The tapestry of the winter's end,
Woven softly, as nights descend.
Threads of snow and whispers cold,
Embroidered stories, silent gold.

Each stitch a memory, faintly spun,
A journey traveled, now just begun.
The colors shift as days grow long,
Nature hums a vibrant song.

In frosted mornings, echoes wane,
Where icy streams break through again.
A patchwork quilt, each piece a tale,
Of seasons changing, winds that sail.

Life emerges from slumber deep,
As winter's watch begins to sleep.
Beneath the surface, warmth ignites,
A tapestry of hope ignites.

The winter's end, a sweet refrain,
Inviting life to bloom again.
In every thread, a promise sewn,
The fabric of the world is grown.

Winter's Embrace

Snowflakes dance in silent air,
Wrapped in warmth, we find our share.
Fires crackle, shadows play,
Winter whispers, night and day.

Cozy blankets, hearts ignite,
Stars above, a twinkling sight.
Beneath the moon's soft silver light,
We hold each other, warm and tight.

Icicles hang like crystal dreams,
Nature's beauty, soft it seems.
Footprints trace in fields of white,
Together we face the chilly night.

Branches bare, a stark display,
Yet love grows in this cold sway.
Seasons change, but we remain,
In winter's grip, we stake our claim.

So let us dance through frosty air,
Wrapped in winter, hearts laid bare.
Each breath a cloud upon the chill,
In winter's embrace, we find our thrill.

Whispering Frost

Gentle winds begin to blow,
Whispering secrets only snow.
Each blade of grass, a frosty kiss,
Nature sleeps in perfect bliss.

Footsteps soft upon the ground,
In the silence, peace is found.
Frosty patterns grace the trees,
Nature's art caught in the breeze.

Winter nights, a velvet cloak,
Embers dance, and fires stoke.
Through the chill, your hand in mine,
Together, love, we intertwine.

Stars above, a guiding light,
In this cold, we find our might.
With every breath, a promise made,
In whispered frost, our fears evade.

The world outside, a tapestry,
Of icy dreams, so wild and free.
Each moment shared, a cherished host,
In winter's arms, we love the most.

Dreams Wrapped in White

Blankets of snow, a world anew,
Each flake a dream, pure and true.
In these moments, we're alive,
In winter's arms, we truly thrive.

Gentle silence, soft and deep,
Nature sings us into sleep.
Under the stars, our wishes fly,
Wrapped in blankets, you and I.

The chill may bite, but hearts stay warm,
In each other's love, we find our charm.
A hush falls down, the world stands still,
With every heartbeat, we feel the thrill.

Candles flicker, shadows dance,
In winter's glow, we take a chance.
Sipping cocoa, laughter flows,
In dreams wrapped white, our love just grows.

Each sunrise paints the horizon bright,
While wrapped in dreams, we hold on tight.
Through frosty mornings, hand in hand,
In winter's spell, we take a stand.

Veils of Ice

Shadows creep, the night is near,
Veils of ice, so stark, so clear.
In the quiet, secrets hide,
Winter calls, we step inside.

Rippling streams, frozen like glass,
Time stands still, as moments pass.
In crystal realms, we lose our way,
Veils of ice hold night at bay.

Each breath a fog against the chill,
Spirits rise, and hearts can fill.
Magic dances in the air,
Copper leaves, a frozen glare.

Whispers linger in the night,
Beneath the moon's soft, silver light.
We walk lightly on frozen ground,
In veils of ice, our love is found.

Together through the frosty haze,
In this moment, we embrace.
With laughter echoing through the trees,
In winter's grip, we find our peace.

The Shape of Winter's Breath

The chill whispers softly, a silent call,
Each breath a mist, in the frosty pall.
Trees stand bare, cloaked in white,
Awaiting dawn's warmth, bathed in light.

Footsteps crunch on the frozen ground,
A world so still, where peace is found.
The sky hangs low, grey and deep,
As nature dreams, in tranquil sleep.

Crystals glisten on branches hung,
A symphony played by winter's tongue.
Winds dance lightly, a whispering song,
In the heart of winter, where we belong.

The stars peek through, a flickering sight,
Guiding lost souls on this wintry night.
With every breath, new stories weave,
In the shape of winter, we hope, believe.

As snowflakes fall, soft and slow,
The world transforms, as dreams bestow.
In the stillness, magic unfurls,
A canvas painted in winter's pearls.

Starlit Paths on Frosty Eves

Beneath a dome of shimmering light,
The world wears frost, all peaceful and bright.
Paths glisten softly, kissed by stars,
Whispers of wonder, from near and far.

Moonlight spills on the silver snow,
Guiding the way where dreams may flow.
Footprints lead to secrets untold,
Stories of magic in the night unfold.

Each twinkle above, a promise made,
In the stillness, worries fade.
Hearts embrace the evening's grace,
As starlit paths we eagerly trace.

Crickets sing their softest tune,
Under the watch of a slumbering moon.
The night wraps us in a gentle fold,
As nature's wonders softly unfold.

Hand in hand, we stroll along,
In frosty eves where we belong.
With every step, the world awakes,
Starlit paths, the heart remakes.

Beneath the Canopy of Winter Dreams

Underneath the frosted sky,
The world rests gently, a tender sigh.
Whispers of dreams drift through the air,
In winter's arms, we find our care.

Snowflakes twirl, a graceful dance,
Painting the earth in a silent trance.
Each breath we take, a fleeting wisp,
As winter wraps us in its crisp grip.

The trees stand tall, adorned in white,
Guardians of dreams in the still of night.
With every shadow, a tale unfolds,
Of warmth and light amidst the cold.

A blanket of silence, peaceful and deep,
Awakening wonders that softly seep.
Beneath this canopy, we find our space,
In the heart of winter's embrace.

With every snowfall, hope is reborn,
In the cradle of twilight, where dreams are worn.
Together we wander, through this serene scene,
Beneath the canopy, our souls convene.

An Ethereal Cloak of Stillness

In the hush of night, soft and deep,
An ethereal cloak drapes over sleep.
A world transformed, calm and bright,
Wrapped in the warmth of winter's light.

The air is crisp, a frosty breath,
Life pauses gently, as if in rest.
Under the stars, secrets are shared,
In stillness, hearts are laid bare.

Patterns in frost weave stories old,
An ancient tale, quietly told.
With each whispering wind that sighs,
Winter's magic dances in the skies.

Footprints vanish, swallowed by snow,
Yet memories linger, sweetly aglow.
Every moment wrapped in grace,
An ethereal cloak, a sacred space.

As dawn breaks softly, the world unveils,
The beauty of winter, its fleeting tales.
In this stillness, we find our way,
Wrapped in wonder, we greet the day.

Soft Crystals on Branches Bare

Soft crystals cling to branches bare,
Glittering whispers float in the air.
Winter's breath weaves a silvery thread,
Painting the world in a frosted spread.

Quiet snowflakes dance from above,
Covering earth like a feathered glove.
Nature's hush sings a tranquil song,
In this frozen realm where we belong.

Each branch wears a delicate crown,
As the daylight fades, shadows drown.
Night wraps the landscape in its shawl,
A serene beauty that enchants all.

Time takes a pause, the moment feels rare,
Inspiring dreams from the crystal flair.
Magic whispers through each frozen sigh,
A world transformed beneath the sky.

Reflections in the Icy Stillness

Reflections shimmer on the lake's glass,
Capturing moments as the seasons pass.
Icy stillness wraps the winter grace,
A mirrored world in this tranquil space.

Whispers of wind brush across the pure,
Nature's embrace feels gentle and sure.
Trees stand tall, their roots deep and wide,
Encased in icicles, secrets they hide.

Footprints of time in the frosty ground,
Echoes of memories lost but found.
Stars above twinkle in icy air,
Silent wishes on a night so fair.

Crystals hang like little lanterns bright,
Guiding the heart through the calm of night.
In the stillness, a promise resides,
Of the warmth that blooms when the cold subsides.

Frost-bitten Memories and Chill

Frost-bitten memories whisper the past,
Each breath a cloud in the chilled steadfast.
Traces of laughter linger like mist,
In the heart of winter, there's warmth still kissed.

The chill wraps around like a lover's embrace,
Holding us close in this quiet space.
Branches adorned with a frosted lace,
Nature's stillness, a beautiful grace.

Time drips slowly, a melting thought,
Moments once treasured, now gently caught.
The pulse of the earth beneath layers of white,
Beats softly, awake in the still of night.

Eyes closed, I journey to days long gone,
In the frosty air, memories dawn.
Fragments of joy, like snowflakes they fall,
In the embrace of chill, I recall them all.

The Enchantment of Dying Light

The daylight fades, an enchanting sight,
Colors bleed into the kiss of night.
Whispers of dusk thread through the trees,
Carried on the softest of breezes.

Flickers of brilliance dance on the stream,
Mirroring stars that begin to beam.
Nature's canvas, a breathtaking view,
Where shadows stretch and dreams come true.

Moments held tightly in dusk's warm glow,
Embers of daylight begin to slow.
In this transition, magic unfolds,
A story of beauty in twilight told.

As night settles deep, the world feels new,
Offering comfort in the night's soft hue.
The enchantment lingers, a sweet refrain,
Carving the heart with its gentle grain.

A Serenade in White

In the hush of winter's night,
Softly falls the snow,
Blanketing the world in white,
Where dreams begin to grow.

Moonlight dances on the glades,
Whispering like a sigh,
While stars in shimmering cascades,
Illuminate the sky.

Footprints trace a quiet path,
Through the drifts so deep,
Nature's song, a gentle wrath,
In winter's tender sweep.

Time slows in this silent realm,
As shadows blend and weave,
An enchanting, endless film,
In which we all believe.

So let us wander hand in hand,
Underneath the starlight,
In this vast, enchanted land,
A serenade in white.

Echoing Through the Pines

In the forest, tall and grand,
Whispers ride the breeze,
Echoes travel, hand in hand,
Dancing through the trees.

Sunlight filters, soft and sweet,
Dappled on the floor,
Every step, a rhythmic beat,
Nature's heart to store.

Birds sing songs of days gone by,
Crickets join the chorus,
As the winds begin to sigh,
Filling hearts with pure bliss.

Mossy carpets, green and lush,
Cover every stone,
In the woods, a calming hush,
Where all can feel at home.

So breathe in the fragrant air,
Let your spirit roam,
In this place, beyond compare,
Echoing through the pines.

Gentle Frost's Caress

Morning breaks with chilled delight,
Frost adorns the leaves,
Glistening in the pale sunlight,
As the world believes.

Each blade of grass, a crystal gem,
Nature's art revealed,
A soft blanket, white and hemmed,
Winter's hand concealed.

Birds take flight on glittered wings,
Chirps of joy they share,
While the beauty winter brings,
Fills the hearts laid bare.

Dance of shadows, light so cold,
Painting scenes anew,
Every moment, pure and bold,
Held in frozen dew.

So let us find the warmth within,
Amid the frosty air,
In this silent, gentle spin,
Of winter's soft caress.

A World Transformed

As dawn breaks, the world awakes,
Colors burst to life,
Every moment, joy it stakes,
Beyond the daily strife.

Mountains rise in misty coils,
Rivers flow with grace,
Nature wearing vibrant spoils,
In this wondrous place.

Fields of gold and skies so blue,
Whispers of the breeze,
Magic lies in every hue,
Carried on the trees.

In gardens lush, and forests deep,
Secrets start to bloom,
Life awakens from its sleep,
Filling every room.

A canvas vast, a world bestowed,
With beauty we create,
In every heart, a story flowed,
A world transformed by fate.

Winter's Veiled Secrets

Whispers in the frosty air,
Snowflakes dance, a gentle prayer.
Beneath the cover, secrets lie,
Waiting for the spring to sigh.

Branches bare, yet life remains,
Hidden warmth in icy chains.
Every flake a story spun,
Tales of winter's quiet fun.

Footprints pressed on glistening ground,
Soft and silent, not a sound.
Echoes of a frosted night,
Wrapped in blankets, pure and white.

Moonlight paints the world so bright,
Guiding dreams through starry nights.
In this hush, the heart can mend,
Winter's touch, a loyal friend.

Now the world holds its breath still,
Nature's pause, a tranquil thrill.
Beneath the chill, the warmth does weave,
In winter's arms, we learn to believe.

Shadows Cast by White

Shadows stretch as sunlight fades,
Whispers through the frosted glades.
Winter's breath, it cools the air,
A quiet world, beyond compare.

Footprints linger on the snow,
Tales of where the wanderers go.
In the dusk, the world transforms,
Beneath the hush, a beauty warms.

Icicles hang from rooftops high,
Glistening like a thousand eyes.
As shadows blend with shades of gray,
Winter calls the light to play.

Branches whisper to the ground,
Nature's secrets all around.
The echo of a snowball's flight,
Crisp laughter, hearts feel light.

In the dark, a soft glow gleams,
Winter's tale unfolds in dreams.
Underneath the frosty sky,
Shadows dance as moments fly.

Embraced by Winter

In winter's arms, the world is still,
Blanketed beneath the hill.
Frosty kisses on the cheeks,
Nature whispers, softly speaks.

Pines wear cloaks of cotton white,
Standing tall in pure delight.
Embers crackle, warmth inside,
A cherished place where hearts abide.

Gentle winds through branches weave,
Breathing stories we believe.
With every snowflake, joy ignites,
Embracing magic, cozy nights.

Stars shimmer in the velvet dark,
While the world awaits a spark.
In the silence, peace descends,
Wrapped in winter, love transcends.

As dawn breaks with frosty grace,
Winter's glow, a soft embrace.
In this season, we find cheer,
In winter's arms, we vanish fear.

Ether of Ice

In the ether of ice, time stands still,
Frozen dreams on the windowsill.
Glistening flakes in dances swirl,
Winter's magic, a gentle pearl.

Silent nights with a moonlit glow,
Secrets through the whispers flow.
Underneath the frosty dome,
Each breath feels like coming home.

Icicles shimmer, a crystal breath,
Nature's art, a kiss of death.
Yet life persists in icy grasp,
In frozen moments, we hold fast.

Dust of snow on branches bare,
Beauty every heart can share.
In this realm of chill and peace,
Worries fade and sorrows cease.

Winter's song, a soothing tune,
Wrapped in silvers of the moon.
Through icy gates, joy will arise,
In the ether, find the skies.

Cascading Crystals

Glistening lights fall with grace,
Whispering stories from space.
Each crystal dances, pure and bright,
A fleeting moment, a pure delight.

In twilight's embrace, they shimmer and glow,
Painting the earth in a delicate show.
Nature's confetti, a sparkling freeze,
A wonder created with effortless ease.

Beneath the moon's watchful gaze,
They twinkle softly, a brilliant haze.
The world adorned in a crystal cloak,
A silent beauty, no words need occur.

As dawn awakens, the sun will rise,
Melting the wonders before our eyes.
Yet in our hearts, their magic stays,
A memory captured in winter's haze.

Fleeting moments, so pure and rare,
Cascading crystals dance in the air.
A magical sight, so hard to forget,
In nature's dream, a timeless duet.

A Journey Through Frost

Step by step, through icy trails,
Whispers of winter tell their tales.
Footprints fading in powdered snow,
A journey awaits where chilly winds blow.

Leaves hang heavy, adorned with white,
Under the soft glow of moonlit night.
Each breath visible, like clouds in the sky,
In this frozen world, I wander and fly.

Branches creak under the frosty weight,
Nature's silence is soft yet great.
Skating on rivers, laughter in air,
The warmth of friendship banishes despair.

Through frozen fields, beneath the stars,
The beauty of winter heals our scars.
A tapestry woven of ice and light,
In a world transformed, everything feels right.

As morning breaks, the chill starts to fade,
A journey painted in frost, unafraid.
With every step, a story unfolds,
In winter's embrace, adventure beholds.

Fables in the Snow

Whispers of winter weave through the pines,
Tales of joy and ancient designs.
Softly they fall, like secrets unspooled,
In the hush of the night, where magic is ruled.

Footprints tell stories of creatures unknown,
Bound in the silence, their tales are sown.
Sparkling stories in flakes now reside,
Carried by breezes, like love that won't hide.

The wind carries hints of laughter and cheer,
Echoes of fables that only we hear.
A snow-covered meadow, a stage for delight,
Where dreams take flight in the shimmering night.

With every flake, old legends arise,
Elders of winter, wise and wise.
In the heart of the storm, they come alive,
Telling their tales through the chill that we thrive.

When spring awakens, and cold meets the sun,
These fables will linger, they're never quite done.
In every snowfall, the stories are cast,
The magic of winter forever will last.

Traces of Winter's Artistry

A canvas of white stretched far and wide,
Nature's brush strokes are hard to hide.
Each flake a masterpiece, crafted with care,
In winter's embrace, beauty laid bare.

Drifts pile high, sculpted by the breeze,
Mountains of snow bring tranquil ease.
Footprints imprint stories untold,
Of laughter and warmth as the season unfolds.

Shadows play beneath branches bare,
Artistry woven in the crisp air.
An intricate quilt stitched with delight,
Hidden treasures revealed in the light.

Frosted patterns on windows aglow,
Reflecting the secrets that only we know.
Each breath crystallizes in the cold air,
Moments immortal, crafted with care.

As the world slumbers, a peaceful sigh,
Traces of magic across the sky.
In winter's realm, art is alive,
A whisper of beauty in each heartbeat's drive.

Frosted Echoes Beneath the Stars

Whispers of winter fill the air,
Silent secrets, softly rare.
Each flake falls, a dance of gold,
Stories in silence, softly told.

The moonlight glimmers on the snow,
A world transformed, in nature's glow.
Footprints trace paths of fleeting time,
Memories linger, pure as a rhyme.

Beneath the stars, the night is calm,
A frosted landscape, a soothing balm.
Echoes of laughter, faint but near,
Carried by winds, sweet and clear.

Time stands still in this frozen space,
Moments captured in nature's embrace.
Dreams wrapped in a quilt of white,
Frosted echoes beneath the night.

With every breath, the cold ignites,
A spark of warmth in starry nights.
In every shadow, a tale is spun,
Frosted echoes, where dreams are won.

Blanket of Silent Dreams

Nestled beneath the night sky's gleam,
Wrapped in a blanket of silent dreams.
Softly drifting, the world serene,
Whispers of magic, a gentle scene.

Stars twinkle bright, like eyes that know,
Stories untold in the soft moon's glow.
Threads of silver in the dark unfold,
Carrying wishes, simple yet bold.

Each breath of night, a sigh of peace,
In the stillness, worries cease.
The world outside, a distant tune,
As dreams take flight beneath the moon.

A dance of shadows, a gentle sway,
In this haven, we drift away.
Wrapped so tight in the evening's seam,
In this moment, we dare to dream.

A blanket woven from starlit threads,
Soft and warm, where heartache treads.
We rise with dawn, but here we stay,
In the silence of dreams, where children play.

The Dance of Flurries

Whirling winds call out to play,
The dance of flurries, a bright ballet.
Twisting and turning under the moon,
Nature's rhythm, a winter tune.

Gentle snowfall, a curtain of white,
Every flake falls, pure and light.
Soft whispers greet the frozen ground,
In the hush, magic can be found.

Children laugh in the chill of the air,
Chasing flurries without a care.
Each swirl and twirl, a fleeting spark,
Painting visions in the dark.

The night wraps close with velvet grace,
As flurries dance in a tender embrace.
Every moment, a cherished delight,
In this winter's waltz, hearts take flight.

The world transforms in a flurry's wisp,
Innocence captured in nature's kiss.
As we twirl beneath the snowy skies,
The dance of flurries, where joy lies.

Chilling Embrace of the Night

The night unfolds with a chilling sigh,
Stars awaken in the darkened sky.
A frosty breath upon the face,
In this moment, we find our place.

Shadows stretch across the ground,
In their depths, solace is found.
The moon reflects on ice-bound streams,
Guiding us softly through twilight dreams.

Whispers echo through the trees,
Carried gently on the winter breeze.
In this stillness, worries take flight,
Embraced by the chill of the night.

Every click of frost on bark,
Signals the secrets hidden in the dark.
Time slows down, the world at ease,
Wrapped so warmly in nature's tease.

A chilling embrace, yet hearts stay warm,
In the night's spell, we are drawn.
With every moment, we hold so tight,
To the chilling embrace of the night.

Glacial Reflections on Time's Surface

In stillness, ice gleams bright,
Capturing moments, frozen light.
Ripples dance on crystal skin,
Whispers of where we've been.

Each crack tells stories long forgot,
Time's currents, a silent plot.
Echoes shimmer in the cold,
History's secrets gently unfold.

Beneath the weight of winter's breath,
Life holds on, defying death.
In this realm of chill and grace,
The heart finds its rightful place.

Reflections blaze in twilight's gaze,
Marking paths through frosted haze.
Echoes of warmth in icy streams,
Within these depths, lie our dreams.

Time suspended in layers thick,
Each moment a timeless flick.
Glacial beauty whispers clear,
Lives entwined, they persevere.

The Quiet Parade of Winter's End

Snowflakes dance on gentle breeze,
Nature stirs with quiet ease.
Underneath the blanket white,
Life prepares for spring's soft light.

Silent shifts in earth and sky,
Winter waves its last goodbye.
Softly melting, colors bloom,
Awakening from frosty gloom.

Branches bare, a stark embrace,
Yet promise lingers in this space.
Each drop that falls, a fleeting song,
Nature hums where we belong.

In the thaw, new hope takes flight,
Tendrils reach for warmer light.
Quiet parades through softening snow,
Winter yielding, time to grow.

Footprints fade, yet life remains,
Nurtured softly by spring's rains.
The quiet march brings joys anew,
In every hue, a world to view.

Chasing Echoes in a Frosty World

In frosted air, clear echoes call,
Whispers soft in the snow's white thrall.
Footsteps crunch on sparkling ground,
In this silence, dreams abound.

Each breath a mist, a fleeting trace,
Chasing shadows, finding space.
Frosted branches, delicate lace,
Nature's canvas, a frozen embrace.

We wander through this icy maze,
Hearts alight with winter's praise.
Where every sound a memory holds,
Stories woven in the cold.

Lingering scents of woodsmoke warmth,
Guiding us through this chilly charm.
With every step, the world transforms,
As frost weaves magic, life conforms.

Chasing echoes, we move along,
In frosty realms where hearts grow strong.
Nature's whispers, a soft refrain,
Bound together through joy and pain.

Nature's Art in Ice Form

Frosted leaves in crystal frames,
Nature sculpts, the world reclaims.
In icy strokes, beauty unfurls,
Artistry in winter's pearls.

Delicate designs, each flake unique,
Nature speaks, the silence speaks.
Patterns form in frozen air,
Curling branches, beyond compare.

Sunlight weaves through winter's art,
Creating warmth from cold's cold heart.
Each glimmer, a moment seized,
In chilling grace, we're all pleased.

Life encased in nature's glass,
Time's reflections as seasons pass.
Painting worlds of white and blue,
A masterpiece, forever true.

Nature's palette, vast and grand,
Crafting beauty with gentle hand.
In every edge, our dreams reborn,
In nature's art, the spirit is worn.

Winter's Womb

In the quiet bend of the night,
Snowflakes fall without a sound.
Moonlight dances soft and bright,
Cradling dreams in frosted ground.

Blankets drape on weary trees,
Nature sleeps in still embrace.
Whispers carried by the breeze,
Time finds solace, gentle grace.

Children laugh in snowy cheer,
Making angels, pure and free.
Each cold breath, a moment dear,
Captured in the memory.

Fires crackle, warmth within,
Stories shared with hearts aglow.
Winter's womb, where dreams begin,
Softly drifting, sweet and slow.

So let the world be hushed tonight,
Wrapped in peace, a crystal dome.
Under stars, a timeless light,
In winter's womb, we find our home.

The Hush of White

Silent streets, a blanket white,
Every sound is hushed and clear.
Footsteps crunching, pure delight,
In the stillness, winter's cheer.

Pines adorned with snowy crowns,
Waves of white across the land.
Nature wears her quiet gowns,
In a world so soft and grand.

The hush of white, a gentle sigh,
Breathing peace in every flake.
Clouds drift slowly through the sky,
In this moment, time can wake.

Warmth lies hidden, hearts embrace,
Mug of cocoa, fires glow.
In the chill, we find our grace,
As the winter winds do blow.

Winter whispers, stories told,
In the night, we lose the fight.
Let the frost, the world behold,
In the beauty of the night.

Frost-kissed Memories

Frost-kissed windows, patterns bright,
Show the world in silver dreams.
Through the chill of winter's night,
Every moment, soft light gleams.

Picnics once beneath the sun,
Now we cherish warmth indoors.
Children laughing, races run,
Echoes linger, fading shores.

Fires crackling in the dark,
Echoes of the year gone by.
In the shadows, love's sweet spark,
Guided by a gentle sigh.

Memory wrapped in frosty lace,
Every breath a heart's embrace.
Time moves slowly, finds its place,
In the lingering winter's grace.

So let the frost remind us all,
Of the warmth that love can bring.
In the quiet, tender call,
Lives the joy of winter's ring.

An Interlude in White

An interlude of frosty glow,
Nature's canvas, pure and bright.
Whispers of the winter snow,
Painting silence in the night.

Footprints lead to paths unknown,
Every journey takes its time.
In the chill, we're not alone,
Finding rhythm, life's sweet rhyme.

Frosty mornings, soft and clear,
Every breath a fleeting cloud.
In this moment, hold it dear,
Underneath the snowy shroud.

Hearts entwined in winter's grasp,
Share the warmth of tender dreams.
Time slows down, a gentle clasp,
As the world in slumber seems.

So let us dance in starlit nights,
In the hush, our spirits soar.
With each flake, a new delight,
In winter's arms forevermore.

Frosted Reverie

In the dawn, the world aglow,
Whispers soft, the cold wind flows.
Trees adorned in sparkling white,
Dreams unfold in morning light.

Crystal flakes that dance and twirl,
Nature's beauty starts to swirl.
A blanket thick with quiet grace,
Time slows down in this embrace.

Footprints trace a silent path,
Guiding whispers of nature's math.
Every flake a story spun,
Underneath the winter sun.

In the hush, a moment rare,
Breath of frost hangs in the air.
Magic lingers all around,
In this peace, true joy is found.

A frosted dream, forever held,
Within the heart where magic dwelled.
Winter's spell, a soft decree,
In this realm, we wander free.

Beneath the Cold Veil

Snowflakes dance on zephyr's breath,
Cloaked in white, the earth finds rest.
Silence echoes, vast and deep,
Beneath the cold, the world does sleep.

Ancient trees with limbs outspread,
Crested crowns like dreams long fled.
Nature's canvas, pure and bright,
Draws us in to winter's night.

Frosty whispers fill the air,
As the moon ascends with care.
Stars align in crystal skies,
Glistening like our hidden sighs.

In this realm of softest light,
Time stands still, the heart feels right.
Moments caught in twilight hues,
Painting dreams for us to choose.

Beneath the veil, we find our way,
In winter's grasp, we long to stay.
Together wrapped in frosty night,
Warmed by love and pure delight.

Echoes of Winter

Whispers low on frosted ground,
Echoes of a world profound.
Snowflakes murmur, soft and light,
Songs of winter take their flight.

Against the hush of icy air,
Dreams are painted everywhere.
Glistening paths where shadows play,
Guide the heart along the way.

In the stillness, moments freeze,
Laughter carried by the breeze.
Footsteps soft as gentle sighs,
In this realm where magic lies.

Fires crackle, warmth bestowed,
Stories shared on winding road.
Huddled close, the hearth aglow,
Echoes whisper tales from long ago.

Winter wraps us in its charms,
Holding closely, safe from harms.
In each echo, joy remains,
Winter's heart, our love sustains.

In the Stillness of Snow

Snow descends, a velvet shroud,
Wrapping all in quiet proud.
In this stillness, breathe it in,
Moments lost, where dreams begin.

Shadows lengthen, twilight glows,
Underneath, the soft wind blows.
Each flake falls, a tale to tell,
In the hush, the heart will swell.

Frozen rivers, still and wide,
Carry echoes of the tide.
Nature rests, tucked away,
In the stillness, night and day.

Hope takes form in feathery white,
Painting all with pure delight.
Here we linger, lost in thought,
In this wonder, love is caught.

So let the snow weave dreams anew,
In its spell, we find our view.
Winter's grace, a soothing balm,
In the stillness, life is calm.

Fractals of Frost

Delicate patterns, drawn with care,
Nature's artistry, beyond compare.
Whispers of winter, softly they glide,
Each flake a secret, a world inside.

Crystals shimmer, reflecting the light,
Dancing and swirling, a breathtaking sight.
Under the sun, they twinkle and glow,
In the quiet dawn, their beauty will show.

Life breathes beneath the icy embrace,
Silent transformations, a slow-motion race.
Every corner, a story unfolds,
Frost-tipped wonders, nature beholds.

As shadows lengthen, the chill takes hold,
The fractals whisper, their tales retold.
In this frozen dance, we find our way,
Lost in the beauty, till the end of day.

Soon spring will come, and all will renew,
Yet in the frost, we find something true.
A fleeting moment, a treasure to keep,
Fractals of frost, in memory deep.

The Quiet of the North

Snow blankets softly, a muffled sound,
Stillness of winter, in silence profound.
The world slows down, wrapped in white,
A tranquil moment, pure and bright.

Trees stand like sentinels, tall and bare,
Guarding the secrets that float in the air.
Each breath a whisper, each step a thought,
In the quiet of the North, peace is sought.

Frozen lakes shimmer, a glassy sheen,
Reflecting the skies, so vast and serene.
Footprints of wildlife, a story to tell,
The beauty of nature, where stillness dwells.

Beneath the bold auroras, colors ignite,
The heavens dance with mesmerizing light.
Every star twinkles in the cold night sky,
In this quiet embrace, we learn how to fly.

With every snowfall, a chance to reflect,
In the quiet of the North, we reconnect.
Here in the stillness, our worries take flight,
Chasing the shadows, igniting the night.

Unraveling Winter's Breath

Softly it whispers, a cool caress,
Winter's breath lingers, an icy press.
Each sigh transforms the world outside,
Nature's slumber, where dreams abide.

Frost-kissed mornings, the dawn breaks clear,
A landscape of glitter, so bright and dear.
Birds take to flight, their silhouettes bold,
While warmth of the hearth keeps stories told.

Crackling firesides, through shadows we share,
Moments together, beyond all compare.
A tapestry woven of laughter and cheer,
The heart beats louder when loved ones are near.

Yet still the chill climbs, a frosty embrace,
Winter's breath dances, leaving a trace.
Unraveling layers, as seasons entwine,
In the heart of the cold, we've come to align.

And though it may wane, this depth of cold air,
The bonds forged in winter, forever we share.
With each melting flake, a memory stays,
Unraveling winter's breath, warming our days.

A Canvas of Silence

Blankets of white stretch far and wide,
A canvas of silence, where secrets reside.
Brushstrokes of snow on the earth's gentle skin,
Nature's soft palette, a hush from within.

Soft flurries fall, like dreams from above,
Wrapping the world in a blanket of love.
Each flake unique, like a wish in the night,
The silence embraces, calm and bright.

Pine trees stand still, their branches adorned,
In the still of the night, a new song is born.
Hoarfrost glistens, like jewels in the dark,
A canvas of silence, where nature will spark.

With every heartbeat, the snow whispers back,
Echoes of winter in trails of white track.
Here in this quiet, our spirits take flight,
Finding our solace beneath the star's light.

When morning arrives, the world comes alive,
Yet in this silence, our dreams will survive.
For in every blank space, beauty is found,
A canvas of silence, where wonders abound.

Milton Keynes UK
Ingram Content Group UK Ltd.
UKHW021400081224
452111UK00007B/106